TRICKS AND STUNTS WITH PLAYING CARDS

Plus Games of Solitaire

(An abridgement of GAMES WITH PLAYING CARDS
Plus Tricks and Stunts)

By
Joseph Leeming

GRAMERCY PUBLISHING COMPANY
NEW YORK

*This edition published by Gramercy Publishing Co.,
a division of Crown Publishers, Inc.,
by arrangement with Franklin Watts, Inc.*

r s t u v w x y z

PRINTED IN THE UNITED STATES OF AMERICA

Contents

♠ ♡ ♣ ◇ ♠ ♡ ♣ ◇ ♠ ♡ ♣ ◇

Contents

SOLUTIONS TO PUZZLES WITH CARDS

20 SOLITAIRES

How We Got Our Pack of Cards

WHEN WE PLAY a card game with an ordinary pack of playing cards we seldom think of the long and fascinating history of these pieces of shiny pasteboard.

The very first playing cards were probably made in China or India many thousands of years ago. From these countries they gradually spread throughout the Far East, and then across the Indian Ocean to Arabia and Egypt.

Playing cards were not known in Europe until about the year 1100 A.D., when a number of packs were brought back from the Holy Land by Crusaders. These knights and their retainers had found that the Saracens of Arabia were familiar with playing cards and spent many hours playing different games with them. The cards that they brought back to Europe were all handmade and had beautiful designs carefully painted by hand.

In some of these packs, a variety of materials was used in addition to paper. Some Oriental cards were made of thin painted sheets of wood, ivory, metal, and even of dried leaves. Canvas, leather, and embroidered silk cards are known to have existed, as well as cards of tortoise shell and small tiles.

As soon as the people of Europe learned about these cards, they began to play all kinds of games with them. By degrees they developed the card designs which were the forerunners of our familiar, present-day cards.

In the early packs of cards, each of the suits represented one of the four social classes of the life of the Middle Ages. The nobility were represented by swords, which later became our Spades. The churchmen were represented by cups, which were later turned into Hearts. The merchant class was represented by coins, which later became Diamonds; and the peasants were represented by staves, which later became Clubs.

The face cards in these early packs contained pictures of actual kings, queens and princes. In many packs the King of Hearts bore the portrait of Charlemagne, while the Jack of Spades had a picture of one of his famous soldiers, a man named Ogier the Dane.

Later, in France, the King of Clubs represented the Pope; the King of Spades the King of France; the King of Diamonds the King of Spain; and the King of Hearts the King of England. The Queen of Spades at that time represented Joan of Arc.

Some of the early playing cards were round in shape, and some were square. It was many years before cards took the easy-to-handle, oblong shape we know today.

Playing cards were first brought to America by the sailors on Columbus's first voyage to the New World in 1492. They took their cards back to Spain with them, however, and it was not until Cortez conquered Mexico in 1521 that playing cards were really introduced into America. After that the other explorers—and there were many of them—brought more packs of cards to this country and card playing became popular in many camps and settlements established in the New World.

Later on, when America began to manufacture its own playing cards, an effort was made to get rid of the Kings and Queens. A picture of George Washington took the place of the King of Hearts, and the card was called the President of Hearts. John Adams, our second president, replaced the King of Diamonds; and Benjamin Franklin and the Marquis de Lafayette (who had come from France to help us win our freedom) replaced the King of Clubs and the King of Spades. The four Queens became the Goddesses of Love, Wisdom, Fortune, and Harvests; and four fierce-looking Indian chiefs took the places of the Jacks.

But this patriotic pack of cards never became really popular. People were too accustomed to the other designs, and soon went back to them.

Some of the cards have romantic or historical associations that are but little known to most people of today. Do you know, for example, which card is known as "the Curse of Scotland"? This is the Nine of Diamonds, which got its strange name in 1746, when the cruel Duke of Cumberland wrote an order on that card, commanding his troops to show no mercy to the Scottish soldiers captured at the Battle of Culloden.

The Six of Hearts, on the other hand, is known to some people as the card of "loyalty at the risk of death." This is because in 1688 an English soldier, Colonel Richard Grace, used this card to write a refusal to surrender and sent it to William of Orange. Colonel Grace was loyal to King James II of England, and risked being shot or hanged for his refusal to give up. The words that Colonel Grace wrote were, "Tell your master I despise his offer, and that honor and conscience are dearer to a gentleman than all the wealth and titles a prince can bestow."

There are other fascinating things about a pack of cards that few people ever stop to think of. As legend says:

The fifty-two cards in the pack correspond with the fifty-two weeks of the year. The thirteen cards in each suit are the same in number as the thirteen lunar or moon months of each year, and also the thirteen weeks in each quarter of the year. In addition: there are four suits, just as there are four seasons in the year. The twelve face, or court, cards correspond with the twelve calendar months of the year.

It is sometimes said that the total value of the cards in the pack, counting Jacks as 11, Queens as 12, and Kings as 13, is 365, or the number of days in a year. This is almost correct, but not quite. The total value of all the cards is 364.

There is an old calculation, however, which comes out to 365. It goes as follows:

Number of pips (spots) on all plain cards .   . 220
Number of pips on all court cards .   .   .   12
Twelve court cards, counted as 10 *each*   .   . 120
Number of cards in each suit   13

    The total equals the number of days in the
      year 365

Card games are played in just about every country in the world today and, to a large extent, games that are very similar are played in different countries. Most of these present-day games are based on old ones that have been played for hundreds of years.

This book contains games that are both old and new, since one of the principal reasons for writing it is to introduce its readers to really good card games, which they may not already know. In selecting these, many people were asked which games they liked the best, and these were included, since experience has shown that they are the most popular.

Readers may find that some games they do already know are presented here with small variations from their own rules. As with many other things, card games have slight changes, or even different names, in different parts of the country. The rules given here seem to be the most widely accepted ones. It is always a good idea before you start playing, however, to be sure that everyone agrees on the rules.

♥

24 STUNTS WITH CARDS

♠

24 Stunts with Cards

♠ ♡ ♣ ◇ ♠ ♡ ♣ ◇ ♠ ♡ ♣ ◇

These stunts with cards, gathered from far and near, can give you hours of fun. Some of them are catches, some are games, and some of them might possibly be classed as puzzles. All are easy to learn and do, and I hope you will have a good time with them.

TOSSING CARDS INTO A HAT

This stunt is like pitching pennies at a wall to see who can get the most pennies closest to the wall. It is good for hours of fun, and people can play it over and over again at different times without getting tired of it.

Open a man's felt hat wide and place it about six feet away from where you are standing or sitting. If you haven't got a hat handy, you can use a shoe box or a basket.

Take a pack of playing cards in your hand and try to flip, throw, or toss the cards into the hat, one at a time. Score 1 for each card that lands in the hat. Let each player go through the pack and the high man will win. Cards that land on the brim count as in if they are not knocked off before the end of the tossing.

There is quite a trick to flicking a card and making it go where you want it to. The best results are usually obtained by holding the cards as shown in the drawing, between the first and second fingers of your right hand. Then curve your wrist back and flip the card on its way with a forward motion of your hand and forearm. If you practice this method, you should be able to get good results and much more accurate direction than by any other means.

MAGNETIZING A CARD

This stunt works best in cold weather, but it usually succeeds in warm weather if you shuffle your feet hard enough. Hold a card in your hand and shuffle your feet along a carpet, moving over toward a wall of the room as you do so. When you reach the wall, slap the card on it and the card will stay there without falling off!

THE FIVE TOUCHING CARDS

Challenge your friends to place 5 cards in such a way that each card will touch each of the 4 other cards.

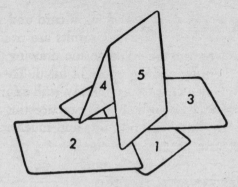

They will undoubtedly fail. You can then proceed to do the stunt by placing the cards as shown in the drawing. It takes a little practice to make the 2 upright cards stand up by leaning them against each other, but it is not really difficult.

AN AMUSING CARD CATCH

Take 5 cards and arrange them as shown in the drawing. Then ask someone if he can take away 2 of the cards, and add 3 cards so that the figure or arrangement of the cards will remain the same.

Better tell your friend that this is a catch, so he will be prepared for what you do. You simply move away the 2 cards at the right and then add the remaining 3 to them.

THE SIX-CARD LIFT

Put 6 cards on the table and then announce that you can lift all 6 of them by picking up one card by the edges while not touching any of the other 5. Make it clear that the stunt is not done simply by pushing one card under the others and then lifting it. When your friends ask how the stunt is done, arrange the cards as shown in the drawing and lift them all by holding the edges of the Ace of Diamonds.

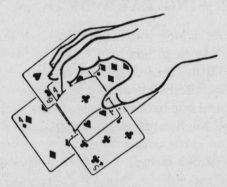

To arrange the cards easily the correct way, first put the card directly under the Ace of Diamonds on the table. Bend the Ace of Diamonds to curve it a little and put it over this card. Put the 2 cards at the right and left over the ends of the Ace of Diamonds. Then put the last 2 cards carefully in place. Each one goes beneath an end of the card under the Ace of Diamonds, but rests on top of the corners of the right- and left-hand cards.

Use old cards if possible, since new ones are so slippery that the cards are likely to slide apart when you lift them.

THE OLD ARMY GAME

This stunt has fooled thousands, and you should have a good time showing it to your friends. Take the 4 Jacks from the pack and put them in a row on the table. Tell your friends they represent four men who decided to enlist in the Army. However, 2 of them, after a physical examination, were rejected while the other 2 were accepted. Ask if anyone can tell which 2 were rejected.

The secret is that on all playing cards made in the United States two of the 4 Jacks have only one eye. These are usually the Jack of Hearts and the Jack of Spades. Very few people notice this, so you can usually baffle your friends.

A SURPRISING CARD DEAL

In this stunt, which your friends will find impossible to do unless you show them how, you take 8 cards from the pack. You then hold the 8 cards in your hand and deal them out in an odd way, alternately dealing one down on the table and putting the next one back *under* the other cards in your hand. Deal until all the 8 cards are on the table, and you wind up with a row of cards, arranged alternately—first a face card, then a plain card, a face card, a plain card, and so on.

The stunt is done by arranging the 8 cards beforehand without letting anyone know. Put 3 plain cards face down on the table. On top of them put 2 face cards, then 1 plain card, then 2 face cards. Put the cards in this order on top of the pack.

When you are ready to show the stunt, take the 8 cards from the top of the pack and lay them helter skelter on the table. Casually pick them up in two's and three's and rearrange them in the right order for dealing, which is the order described above. Tell your friends to watch closely. Then deal the cards as described above.

ONE CARD UNDER THE OTHER

This is a good gag, which always produces a laugh. Put a King and a plain card on the table. The problem is to move the plain card under the King without touching the King. This seems impossible until you take the plain card and hold it under the table directly under the spot where the King is.

THE MASTER AIM

Put a hat on the floor, ask a friend to stand directly over it with a pack of cards in his hand, and try to drop the cards one at a time into the hat. He should drop the cards from about the height of his waist.

Most of the cards will undoubtedly miss the mark and flutter away to the side of the hat as indicated in Fig. 18.

Fig. 18

Fig. 19

You can then show him your master aim by dropping the cards fairly and squarely into the hat. Simply hold them flat, as shown in Fig. 19, and drop them in that position instead of on edge as almost everybody does.

TO MAKE FOUR FIVES EQUAL 16

Take the 4 fives from the pack and ask if anyone can lay them out so as to total 16. This seems impossible, but there is a solution and a good one. Simply overlap each card as shown in the drawing and the trick is done.

THE THIRTY-CARD RACE

This is a stunt that you can always win, to the utter bewilderment of your friends who don't know how it is worked. What you do is to deal 30 cards onto the table. Then you and a friend take turns picking up cards. At each turn a player can take any number of cards he wants—from 1 through 6. The winner—who is always yourself—is the one who captures the last notch.

Secret: To win, you must pick up enough cards to be the first to reach these three key numbers: the ninth, the sixteenth and the twenty-third cards. After 23, no matter how many cards your friend takes, he must leave the last one for you.

One way to help you count and always take the right number of cards is to remember that after you reach the first key number, 9, the number of cards your friend takes, plus yours, must always equal 7.

It doesn't matter who is the first to start. If you start, however, always take 2 cards. Then, no matter how many cards your friend takes—from 1 through 6—you can always pick up the ninth card.

THE ONE-TWO-THREE CARD RACE

This is another card race, in which 15 cards are used. You and a friend take turns picking up 1, 2 or 3 cards at each turn. In this race, the idea is *not* to get stuck with the last card. The person who takes the last card is the loser. It is never you.

Secret: Either person can start, although it's easier to win if you do. You will win if after each turn you leave 13, 9 or 5 cards on the table.

If you start, take 2 cards, leaving 13. If your friend starts and you miss out on 13 and 9, catch up on your third turn and leave 5 cards on the table.

MAKING A CARD INVISIBLE

Take a card from the pack and tell one of your friends that you can bewitch him in such a way that the card will be invisible to him, even though the other people in the room will be able to see it.

When you are told that this seems unlikely or even impossible, put the card on top of your friend's head.

STANDING A CARD ON EDGE

Take a card from the pack and ask some friend if he thinks he can stand it upright on one edge. Your friend will probably try, but will find that it just can't be done.

You then proceed to do the stunt by simply bending the card to make it curved, as in the drawing.

THE WHISPERING QUEEN

This is a stunt that is done by two people who are in "cahoots" with each other—that is, they know the secret, but nobody else does. You and a friend do it together at a party or some other gathering.

He is to stay in the room while you go into the next room. When you are gone, he holds up the Queen of Hearts facing someone, so the Queen can have a good, close look. He then tells you to come in, and gives you the Queen. You hold the card close to your ear so it can whisper the name of the person it looked at, and then you name the person. Everyone is pretty surprised, but the principle is very simple.

Your friend signals the right person to you by sitting or standing in the same position. If the person is sitting up straight with hands folded, your friend does the same. If the person has his legs crossed, your friend crosses his, and so on. After a little practice, two people can usually master this stunt so that it never fails.

YOU CAN'T LOSE

Give a friend a pack of cards and ask him to remove a number of them, and count them secretly to see if he has an odd or even number of cards. When this is done, take a few cards from the pack yourself. Then tell your friend that when your cards are added to his, the total number of cards will be an even number, if he has an odd number of cards, or an odd number, if he is holding an even number of cards.

You can't lose. You always take an *odd* number of cards— 3, for example—from the pack. If these are added to an odd number such as 5, the total will be an even number, 8. If they are added to an even number, such as 4, the total will be an odd number, 7.

COIN ON CARD STUNT

If you can get several friends all trying to do this stunt at once you can have a barrel of fun. Balance a card on the second finger of your left hand. Then take a coin and place it on top of the card directly over the tip of your second finger, as in the drawing. The stunt is to remove the card without touching or dropping the coin.

It all depends on how deft you are. Just flick the card with the first or second finger of the right hand, striking it right at the end of one of the corners. The card will fly away in a whirling motion and, if you are good, the coin will drop directly on the second finger of the left hand.

CARD CROSS STUNT

It's surprising how many people you can puzzle with this stunt. Most people will believe it isn't possible until you show them how to do it.

Arrange 6 cards in the form of a cross, as shown in the drawing. Then ask a friend if he can move 1 card to make the cross have 4 cards in each crosspiece.

The stunt is done by picking up the bottom card of the vertical row and putting it on top of the second card from the top. Each crosspiece will then contain 4 cards, though not in the way your friend may have expected.

ALL IN ORDER

In doing this card-dealing stunt, you take 13 cards from the top of the pack and deal them as follows:

Hold the 13 cards in your hand, face down. The rest of the pack is not used. Put the top card in your hand, under the 12 others, face down. Put the next card on the table, face up. Put the next one under the order cards, the next one on the table, and so on until all 13 cards are on the table. The surprising thing is that the cards are in numbered order, and run in sequence from the Ace up to the King!

To do the stunt, arrange the cards beforehand. Put the Ten face down on the table. On top of it put, face down, the Six, King, Five, Nine, Four, Jack, Three, Eight, Two, Queen, Ace and Seven. Keep the cards in this order and put them face down on top of the pack.

When you are ready to begin, remove these pre-arranged 13 cards and deal them as described above. The effect is quite uncanny as, one after the other, the cards come out in numerical order.

If your friends think the stunt is easy to do, give them the thirteen cards and let them try it!

A BAFFLING CARD STUNT

This stunt has always been a favorite of mine; I have used it many times and had a lot of fun with it. Few people ever catch on to it.

Ask a friend to take any number of cards up to 15 from a pack, to count the cards, but not to let you know how many he has. You then take some cards, always being sure to take more than 20. Just count your cards off silently. We will assume that you took 23 and that your friend took 14 cards, although you do not know or need to know the number he has.

Now you say, "I have as many cards as you have, and enough more to make 19 and 4 over." Both of you start counting your cards onto the table. When he reaches 14, he will put down his last card. Then you repeat, "I said I had enough more to make 19—that means 5—" and you count 1, 2, 3, 4, 5 cards onto the table, "and 4 cards left over," and you show the 4 cards in your hand.

The explanation of this is simplicity itself. All you do is to say that you have 23 cards, but you say it in such a way that everybody is mystified. When you say that you have enough more cards to make 19 and 4 over, you are saying that you have 19 plus 4 cards, or 23 cards. You could also say "I have enough more to make 18 and 5 over," or "to make 17 and 6 over," always starting with some number over 15, which is the most your friend can have.

Try it out with a friend and you will see how baffling a stunt it is.

WHAT'S ON YOUR MIND?

This stunt is always good for a laugh, especially if you show it to some friend when there are other members of your gang present.

You deal 6 cards face down from the top of the pack, dealing 1 to your friend, 1 to yourself, 1 to your friend, 1 to yourself, and so on until you each have 3 cards. Then you ask your friend, "What's on your mind?" It doesn't matter what he replies. You tell him that you are sure you know what is really on his mind and that you have dealt him cards that reveal the secret. He turns up the cards, and they are 3 Queens!

You pick the cards up and say, "Well, let's try it again. Maybe it will come out different!" But, each time your friend gets 3 Queens, and you can keep it up as long as you like, dealing him 3 Queens time after time.

To arrange the cards for this stunt, you take the 4 Queens and put them face down on top of the pack with 1 ordinary card among them. From the top down, the cards should be arranged in this order: 3 Queens, the ordinary card, then the fourth Queen. The sixth card will be the next card on the pack—it doesn't matter what it is.

Now take the pack face down in your left hand, deal the top card face down to your friend, the next one face down to yourself, and so on. He will have 3 Queens. While he is looking at them, slip the top card of your 3 face-down cards to the bottom, beneath the other 2. Put your 3 face-down cards on the pack, then put your friend's 3 Queens face down on top of them. Then deal again and he will once more get 3 Queens.

You can continue to deal as long as you like, with the same result, by always putting your top face-down card under your two other face-down cards, and putting your friend's Queens on top of them.

THE ELEVENS STUNT

Tell your friends that you can put 3 cards on the table as often as you wish to form numbers that can be divided evenly by 11 without leaving any remainder. Then challenge them to see if they can figure out how you do it.

The drawing shows an example—a Three, an Eight and a Five, forming the number 3 8 5. Divide 11 into 385 and it goes 35 times exactly. You can do this over and over with different groups of cards, and your friends will have a mighty hard time guessing the secret.

The secret is always to have the values of the first and third cards add up to the value of the middle card. Thus, in the drawing, the Three and the Five add up to Eight.

BUILDING CARD CASTLES

Building card castles takes steady hands and a good deal of patience. But the results are worth it, if you are successful. You can build castles four, five or even six stories high if you can balance the cards accurately and steadily.

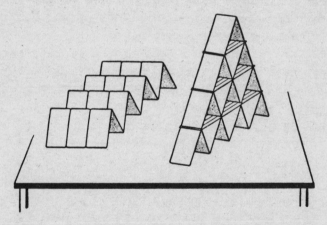

If you have never tried to make a card castle, the drawing will show you what one looks like. They are made by resting pairs of cards against each other at an angle.

The first story may consist of a single row of three or more pairs of cards. When these are in place, you lay a floor of cards on top of them. Then you build a second story by balancing more cards together on the floor and, if you can, you go on to add additional stories until you have room for only one pair of cards at the top of the castle.

Very often, of course, some pair of cards will give way, and the whole building will come tumbling down before it is completed. Then you just pick up the cards and start all over again from the beginning.

When you get really good at building with cards, try making a first story of three or four rows, each row containing three or four pairs of balanced cards. Roof this over with cards, laid flat to form an oblong or square platform, and go on building on top of it.

SPELLING BEE

Here is another dealing-out stunt that is first rate: Hold 13 cards in your hand and deal them, spelling out the numbers of the cards, 1 card for each letter. At the end, all 13 cards lie beside each other on the table, arranged in proper numerical order or sequence.

Begin by spelling A-C-E, and as you say each letter, put the top card at the bottom of the packet of 13 face-down cards in your hand. Then put the next card face up on the table. It's an Ace.

Then spell T-W-O, putting a card under the packet for each letter, and then put the next card face up on the table. It's a Two. Keep on in the same way, spelling out T-H-R-E-E and putting the next card on the table and so on right up through the Jack and Queen. Then the King is the only card left in your hand, and you place it on the table.

At the end, all 13 cards lie beside each other, arranged in proper numerical order or sequence.

To do this stunt, the 13 cards of one suit are arranged as follows: Put the Five face down on the table. On top of it put face down the Nine, Ten, King, Jack, Two, Four, Six, Queen, Ace, Seven, Eight and Three.

Then deal as described above, and you can't miss.

◆

17 MAGIC TRICKS WITH CARDS

◆

17 Magic Tricks with Cards

♠ ♡ ♣ ◇ ♠ ♡ ♣ ◇ ♠ ♡ ♣ ◇

This section contains seventeen of the best magic card tricks that have dramatic effects and that are easy to do. None of them requires sleight of hand. All of them are good. If you learn some of them and practice them well, you should be able to acquire a real reputation as a wizard. For the best results, do not give away the secrets of how the tricks are done.

TELLING A CHOSEN CARD

Ask someone to draw a card from the pack and look at it without showing it to anyone else. Ask him to multiply the value of the card (the number, if it is a plain card, of its spots) by 3, add 6 to the product, then divide the last answer by 3. Tell him to give you the result. Then subtract 2 from that number and you will be able to tell him the value of his card.

The Aces count as 1, Jacks count as 11, the Queens as 12, and the Kings as 13.

Example. Supposing your friend drew a Ten. He multiplies it by 3 and gets 30. He adds 6 and gets 36. He divides this by 3 and gets 12, which is the number he tells you. You subtract 2 from 12 and say:

"Your card is a Ten!"

THE REVERSED CARD

This trick is a very mystifying one, although the key to the mystery is always right before the eyes of the people to whom you show it. To do it, put 5 or 6 cards on the table in a row, as in the drawing. Then turn your back to the cards and ask someone to turn upside down any card he pleases—not face-down but simply around so the top and bottom ends change places. He does so and you turn to the cards, concentrate for a moment, and point out which card has been reversed or turned around.

The trick is done by using cards that magicians call "pointers." In every pack there are a number of cards that have more spots pointing in one direction than in the other. The drawing above shows a few of these "pointers." There are others that you can easily find by looking through the pack.

Before you do the trick you select some of these cards and put them on top of the pack, making sure that all point in the same direction. Lay them out, without turning them, and notice which way they all point. Then, when someone reverses a card, you can easily discover it.

You can also use the "pointer" cards to tell what card a person draws from the pack. Arrange a pack containing only the pointers, and have them all pointing one way. After someone draws a card, reverse the pack, and have the card put back in it. Then deal the cards out face up on the table. The card which is pointing the wrong way is the chosen one.

CUT THE PACK

This method of telling a chosen card has been used by many professional magicians and is well worth learning. It is mystifying and it requires absolutely no sleight of hand.

Shuffle a pack of cards thoroughly and just as you finish, glance at the top card. If this seems hard to do without being detected, just hold the pack face up in one hand and run the cards over into your other hand as though looking casually through the pack. While you are doing this, it is easy to see and memorize the top card.

Give the pack to someone and ask him to put it face down on the table and cut it into two piles. Pick up the pile that formed the bottom part of the pack and put it on the rest of the cards at right angles as in the drawing.

Now talk for a moment, saying that the pack was cut wherever the spectator wished and that you, of course, have no way of knowing what card it was cut at. This is simply to let a moment or two go by so the spectators will forget which was the top and which the bottom part of the pack.

Ask someone to pick up the top half and to look at the top card of the bottom half. This is the card you know. It was the top card of the pack at the start. Now you know the "chosen" card and can name it right away.

THE LIE-DETECTOR TRICK

Tell your friends that you have developed to an uncanny degree your ability to tell whether or not a person is telling the truth. This came about, you might add, after many long years of study in the Orient. Be that as it may, this is a good card trick, and this is how it is done.

As you shuffle the cards or hold them in your hands, look at and remember the fourth card from the top of the pack. Let's say it is the Three of Hearts. Now cut the pack into 3 piles on the table. Take 4 cards off the pile that was on top of the pack. Deal out a card on top of each of the 3 piles and give the fourth card to a spectator. This is the Three of Hearts, but no one knows that you know it.

Now have the spectator replace the card in any one of the piles, put the piles together, and shuffle the cards as much as he wants to. Then ask him to deal out the cards face up one at a time, while he says "Yes" or "No" for each card. His idea is to make it impossible for you to tell if he is naming the chosen card. You don't care, however, for when you see the Three of Hearts you say it is the chosen card, even though the dealer may have said "No." Nothing can beat that old Oriental lie-detecting system.

INSTANTANEOUS REVERSAL

This is a trick that will make your friends think you are a master of sleight of hand. It really works itself.

Before you start, put the Seven of *Clubs* and the Eight of *Spades* in the pack reversed so that they are face up, as shown in the drawing. When starting the trick, run through the cards and pick out the Seven of *Spades* and the Eight of *Clubs*.

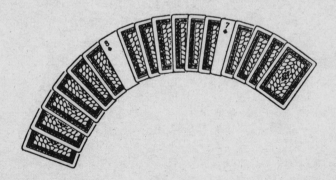

Hold these up and say, "Now watch me closely. The hand is quicker than the eye." You say this to avoid saying, "Here is the Seven of Spades and the Eight of Clubs." Just let the spectators look at the cards. Then proceed.

Put the 2 cards face down into the face-down pack. Snap your fingers at the pack and spread it out face down. The spectators will see the two other cards face up and because the cards are so alike they will think that you have turned them over by sleight of hand.

MYSTIC TAPPIT

Arrange 12 cards running from an Ace to a Queen in the form of a clock dial, as shown in the drawing. Then ask someone to think of one of the cards but not to tell you which one it is.

Now tell your friend that as you tap your pencil on the cards he is to count the taps silently, but is to begin with the number next higher than the card he chose and count up from there. For example, if he selected a Five, he would count your first tap as 6, your second tap as 7, and so on. Tell him to say "Stop" when his count reaches 20, and that you will tell him which card he secretly selected.

Secret: First tap the Seven, then the Six, than the Five, and so on around the circle of cards. If you do this, your pencil will always be tapping the chosen card when your friend says "Stop."

SURE WAY TO FIND A CHOSEN CARD

Every amateur magician should know this professional secret. With it you can let a person draw any card from a pack and you can always find the card.

The secret is this. Simply look at and remember the bottom card of the pack. Have a person take a card, look at it, and replace it on the top of the pack. Then cut the cards, putting the bottom half on top; this puts the bottom card, which you know, directly on top of the chosen card. The cards can then be cut many times, but whenever you want to reveal the chosen card, it will be waiting for you directly below the card that was originally the bottom card.

FOUR-ACE PRODUCTION

You can perform the small miracle of producing the 4 Aces from the pack after it has been shuffled and placed in your coat pocket, if you follow the method given here.

Before doing the trick, secretly remove the 4 Aces from the pack and put them in your right-hand coat pocket. Then let anyone shuffle the pack thoroughly. Take the pack and put it in your pocket, putting it outside of the Aces.

Tell the spectators that your little finger is extraordinarily sensitive and can tell an Ace immediately by touch. Then reach into your pocket and bring out the Aces one at a time.

THE THREE FRIENDLY QUEENS

Take 3 of the Queens from a pack and hand them to a friend. Ask him to put them back in the face-down pack, one on the top, one in the middle, and one on the bottom. He is then to cut the pack several times, putting the bottom half on the top half. Despite this mixing-up, the Queens are such friends that when you run through the pack face up, they are found together.

Secret: As you look for the 3 Queens at the beginning of the trick, slip the fourth Queen on the bottom of the pack. Then, when the cards are cut, 3 Queens will be brought together. The sharpest eyes fail to notice the change in the suit of one of the Queens—that one being the fourth Queen secretly placed on the bottom of the pack.

THE THREE-CARD ANSWER

Ask a friend to take from the pack 3 cards that are in successive order, such as Two, Three and Four, or Six, Seven and Eight. When he has done this, ask him to arrange them

in a row, without your seeing them, so that the highest card is on the left, the next highest in the middle and the lowest on the right, as in the drawing.

Suppose he picks a Six, a Seven and an Eight. He puts them in a row, which makes the number 876. Ask him to reverse their order in his mind and to subtract the number they then make from the number they made in the original order. He does this and subtracts 678 from 876, using pencil and paper.

You then look through the pack and remove 3 cards. "Is this the answer?" you ask, holding up the 3 cards. Yes, it is the answer, and you always guess it correctly.

Here's how it's done. The answer will always be 198. All you have to do is remove an Ace, a Nine and an Eight, arrange them in order, and the trick is done.

A FAMOUS FOUR-ACE TRICK

This is a simple and easily done card mystery, but a very baffling one.

Take the 4 Aces from the pack and give them to someone to hold. You then ask him to put 1 Ace on top of the pack, 1 on the bottom, and the remaining 2 in the middle. You then cut the pack several times and spread out the cards or deal them onto the table. All 4 Aces are found together!

TOP HALF   BOTTOM HALF

The trick is done as follows. As soon as the first 2 Aces have been put on the top and bottom, put the pack on the palm of your left hand and cut it into halves, as shown in the drawing. Immediately pick up the bottom half with your right hand. Then ask your friend to put the remaining 2 Aces on top of the top half. When he has done this, put the bottom half on top of the rest of the cards, and the 4 Aces will all be together. You can then cut the pack as often as you wish and the Aces will not be separated.

THE GREAT "STOP!" TRICK

This trick is a stunner! Be sure to learn it. You give a pack of cards to a friend and ask him to deal onto the table 6 piles face down in a row, adding 1 card to each pile on each round of dealing from left to right. He is then to take a card from the middle of any pile, look at it, replace it face down on top of the pile, then put the rest of the piles on top, and cut the cards several times.

You then ask him to deal out the cards one at a time, naming each card. When he comes to his chosen card you say, "Stop! You just dealt your card." And it always is. The great part of this trick is that you never touch or go near the cards from start to finish, which makes it seem impossible to do.

Secret: This is really clever. Before doing the trick, remove 4 Sevens or any other 4 cards of the same value from the pack, so 48 cards remain, 12 in each suit. Then put 6 cards of one suit—Hearts, for example—on top of the pack, and 6 more Hearts on the bottom. Thus, when your friend deals the cards out into 6 piles, face down from left to right, there will be a Heart at the bottom of each of his piles and a Heart on the top.

When he takes a card and puts it on top of a pile, he puts it on top of a Heart. When he puts another pile on top of the first one, he puts another Heart on top of his chosen card. Thus, his card is the only one in the pack that is sandwiched in between 2 Hearts. When he deals out the cards and says, for example, "Three of Hearts, Eight of Clubs, Nine of Hearts," you will know that his card must be the Eight of Clubs.

MAGIC CARD REVELATION

Give someone a pack of cards and ask him to pick a card and hold it up so that everybody, including yourself, can see it. You then take back the pack, put it in your coat pocket, and say, "Now watch this closely. I am going to draw out cards from the pack that will match the chosen card. The trick is done by my educated little finger."

Suppose the chosen card is the Nine of Hearts. You reach into your pocket and bring out an Eight and an Ace which, added together make 9. Then you reach in again and bring out a Heart to match the suit of the chosen card.

How do you do it? Well, here's the secret. Before starting the trick you put 4 special cards in your pocket. These are the Ace of Diamonds, Two of Spades, Four of Hearts and Eight of Clubs. With these 4 cards you can match the number and the suit of any card in the pack. Try it and you'll see how it works. But be sure that you remember the order of the special cards in your pocket so that you can always bring out the one you want.

INSTANT CARD LOCATION

Sometimes the simpler a card trick is, the more it fools your friends. This is a trick of that kind. You take a pack of cards and cut it into halves. Then you have someone choose 2 cards from one heap, look at them, and put them into the other half of the pack. Ask him to shuffle thoroughly the half into which he has put the cards. You take the half from him after the shuffling and immediately pick out the cards he selected.

The secret of this trick lies in the fact that you have separated the cards beforehand. In one half you have put all the even cards like Two, Four, Six, Eight, Ten and Queen. All the others go into the "odd" half—all odd numbers like Ace (1), Three, Five, Seven and so on. Then all you need to do to discover the chosen cards is to look at the half of the pack into which they were put. If it is the "odd" half, the chosen cards will be the only even ones in it, and vice versa.

To make it easy to cut the pack into the two halves, curve the upper half a little as shown in the drawing.

HIT THE DECK

Ask someone to choose a card, memorize it and replace it on top of the pack without your seeing what the card is. You then cut the cards, putting as usual, the bottom part of the pack on the top part, and tell your friend that to make the trick work you want him to "hit the deck." (Deck is another word used for a pack of playing cards.) Hold the cards in your hands and have him hit them several times.

Then spread out the cards face down. The hitting has apparently reversed one card, for there is a card face upward in the pack. "Aha," you say, "the trick has worked," and you immediately draw out the chosen card from the face-down pack.

The preparation for this trick before it is shown is turning face up the fifth card from the bottom of the pack. Then, when your friend takes a card, replaces it on the top of the pack, and the pack is cut, the chosen card will be the fifth card beneath the face-up card. Having your friend "hit the deck" is just a bit of diversion to make it harder to guess how the trick is done.

THE MAHATMA MARVEL CARD TRICK

This trick is so impossible to detect that it is named for the mahatmas or master magicians of the Orient. Yet it is so easy to do that you can learn it in a few moments.

You give a well-shuffled pack of cards to a friend and ask him to count down from the top any number between 1 and 10 and remember the card at that number. He is also to remember the number of cards it is from the top—the third, fourth, fifth or some other number. He is then to cut the cards so that nobody will know the location of the secretly chosen card.

Next you ask your friend to deal the cards on the table from left to right in the same number of piles as the number of cards his chosen card was from the top, adding 1 card to each pile on each round of dealing. For example, if he chose the third card from the top he would deal the cards out into 3 piles. If his card was the fifth from the top, he would deal the cards into 5 piles, and so on.

When this has been done, ask your friend to pick up the piles—in any order—and to give them all to you. Then, by simply looking through the cards, you can immediately find the chosen one.

All you have to do is to look at and remember the bottom card of the pack at the start of the trick. Then proceed just as described above. When your friend deals the cards onto the table in the same number of piles as the number his card was from the top, he automatically causes the bottom card and the chosen card to come together. It's hard to believe but it's true.

When you look through the cards held face up and spread out from left to right in your hand, the card just to the right of the original bottom card will be the chosen card.

MIRACLE SPOT REVELATION

This is not "just another trick." It is a card trick known to professional magicians and used by them. Its effect is dramatic and it requires no sleight of hand. I have done it hundreds of times and I would urge you to learn it because you will enjoy doing it.

The effect is, briefly, that you deal a pack of cards face down into a number of piles on the table. You ask someone to choose 3 of the piles. This is done, and you then ask your friend to turn 2 of the 3 piles face up. The third pile is left face down, but you immediately name the number of spots on its bottom card. The pile is turned face up—and you are always right!

This is how you do it: Take the pack of cards in your hand. Lift off the top card and show it. Suppose it is a Six. Put it on the table, face down. Then begin to count from the number of the card—in this case, six. Put a card from the pack on the first card, face down, and say "Seven." Continue this until you have counted to ten. This makes a pile of 5 cards.

Now turn up the next card of the pack and do the same thing, starting to count from whatever its number may be. Put this card face down, beside the first pile, and count up to ten as before, adding a card for each number counted.

Repeat this process of counting to ten from whatever number the turned-up card is until you have no more cards in your hand.

The face cards—King, Queen and Jack—and also the Tens, are put by themselves in one pile. If you turn up one of these cards, put it aside by itself. Then, if you turn up others, put them on top, all in the same pile.

When all the piles are completed, pick up all that contain

less than 4 cards. Also pick up the last pile you dealt out, unless it came out even on the count of ten. Even though it may contain more than 4 cards, pick up this pile, unless it made an even ten. Put the piles you pick up to one side, and on top of the face cards and Tens you have put to one side.

Now ask your friend to select 3 of the piles. When he has done this, ask him to pick up all the other piles and give them to you. Take these cards and add them to the cards you have piled together. This leaves only the 3 chosen piles on the table.

Run the cards of the pile you have put to one side from one hand to the other, and count off silently 19 cards. Put these down. Then ask your friend to turn over 2 of the 3 chosen piles. Assume that the bottom cards are a Three and a Four, as in the drawing. Add these together to get 7. Then remove 7 cards from those remaining in your hand.

The number of cards left in your hand will now tell you the number of spots on the bottom card of the third chosen pile. If you have 3 cards left, the card is a Three, and so on. Announce the number of spots. Then turn the pile over and reveal the hidden card.

This trick works on a mathematical principle and will always succeed if you do each move properly.

25 PUZZLES WITH CARDS

25 Puzzles with Cards

♠ ♡ ♣ ◇ ♠ ♡ ♣ ◇ ♠ ♡ ♣ ◇

(See answers on page 63.)

CHANGING THE ROWS

Take 8 face cards from the pack, and 8 of the lower cards such as Threes, Fours and Fives. Then arrange them in 4 rows on a table, alternately, 4 in a row, as shown in the drawing (Fig. 20).

Fig. 20

The puzzle now is to move 2 cards to different positions so that every card can be in a row consisting entirely of face cards or entirely of lower cards. The first or left-hand row will be all face cards, the second row all lower cards, the third row all face cards, and so on.

There is a little catch to this, so be prepared for it. The rows in the solution don't necessarily have to be straight up-and-down and across.

THE ADD-TO-18 PUZZLE

This is one of the puzzles that you can figure out without too much difficulty if you work at it a bit.

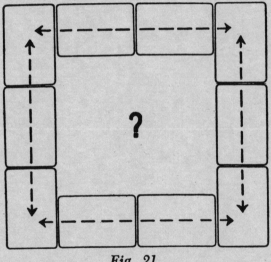

Fig. 21

The puzzle is to take 10 cards from a pack, beginning with an Ace and up to and including a Ten, and then see if you can arrange them in a hollow square like the one shown in the drawing (Fig. 21) so that the spots on the cards forming the four sides add up to 18 for each one of the 4 sides. The spots on 4 cards are to be added together in the top and bottom rows, and the spots on 3 cards in the side rows.

THREE-IN-A-ROW

Put 3 cards—any cards will do—in a row on the table. Then see if you can remove the middle card from its central position without touching it.

THE SIXTEEN-CARD PUZZLE

Take all the Kings, Queens, Jacks and Aces from a pack of cards—16 cards all told. Then see if you can arrange the 16 cards in 4 rows of 4 cards each, so that no 2 of the same suit or of the same value are in any one 4-card row—up and down, straight across, or diagonal.

ALTERNATE CARDS

Arrange 4 face cards and 4 of the plain cards alternately in a row, as shown in the drawing (Fig. 22). The puzzle then

Fig. 22

is to move 2 adjacent cards (2 that are next to each other) at a time and in 4 such moves to bring all the face cards together at one end of the row and all of the plain cards together at the other end of the row.

THE FIVE-KINGS PUZZLE

Put any 10 cards in a row face down on the table, as shown in the drawing (Fig. 23). What you must then try to do is to pick up a card, jump it over 2 cards next to it—to left or right—and make a king of the next or third card—a king being 2 cards, one on top of the other, as in checkers.

Fig. 23

Then you must keep on jumping over 2 cards at a time in the same way until all the cards are arranged 2 together as kings. When you jump over a king, you are to consider it as 2 cards. You can jump both to the right and the left, and there are 5 jumps in all.

THE NOBLE LORDS AND THE COMMONERS

Take from the pack 6 face cards, which we are here calling the "noble lords"; and at the same time remove 6 plain (or

Fig. 24

spot) cards, which in this puzzle represent the "common people." Arrange the cards as shown in the drawing (Fig. 24) so that the noble lords and commoners are mixed up together in the rows.

Now, by touching only 1 card, see if you can make the top row and the third row from the top all noblemen, and the second and fourth rows all commoners. There is a little catch to this, so see if you can find it out.

TRICKY TRIANGLE

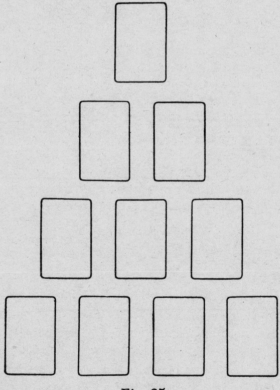

Fig. 25

Make a triangle like the one in the drawing (Fig. 25) using any 10 face-down cards from the pack. Then see if you can turn the triangle upside down—so that it is pointing down instead of up—by moving 3 of the cards.

FACE-UP

Put 3 cards on the table in a row. The 2 end cards are turned face down, and the center card is face up (Fig. 26).

Fig. 26

The puzzle now is to make 3 moves, turning over 2 cards at each move, and finish with all 3 cards face up.

THE STAR PUZZLE

Take any 10 cards from the pack and put them in a heap on the table. Then see if you can arrange them to form a star, made up of 5 lines or rows of 4 cards each.

THE JEALOUS KINGS

Take from the pack the King and Queen of Clubs, the King and Queen of Hearts, and the King and Queen of Diamonds. These represent three happily married couples; but the Kings, or husbands, are all very jealous men.

One day they all went out walking together and came to a river. There was only one boat in which they could get across, and it would hold only two people at a time. The Kings said that no King could be with a Queen unless her husband (the King of the same suit) was present, either on land or in the boat.

How, under these circumstances, did they cross the river in the boat?

Take the 6 cards and see if you can move them across an imaginary river on your table, so that no Queen is ever with a King of another suit unless the King of her own suit is with her.

THE HOURGLASS PUZZLE

Take cards with spots numbering from 1 (an Ace) up to 7 from the pack. Then see if you can arrange them in the hour-

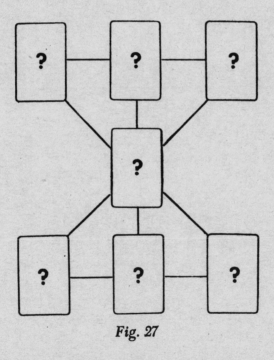

Fig. 27

glass pattern shown in the drawing (Fig. 27) so that the spots on the cards in each 3-card row—straight across, up and down, and diagonal—add up to 12.

THE EIGHTEEN-CARD CIRCLE

This is a good deal like the Hourglass Puzzle, but is harder.
You need 11 cards, ranging from an Ace up to a Jack. The
value of the Jack is 11.

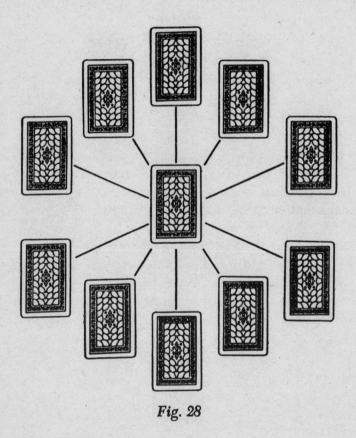

Fig. 28

See if you can put one card in the center and the other 10
cards around it in a circle (Fig. 28), so that the spots of every
line or row of 3 cards stretching from one side of the circle
through the center to the other side will add up to 18.

A CARD BRAIN-TWISTER

This is a puzzle that you can figure out, but you have to be really pretty good to guess it. Take the statements one by one, figure out each one's possibilities, and see how well you can do.

Fig. 29

The drawing (Fig. 29) shows the backs of 3 playing cards. There is at least one Three just to the right of a Two. (That means that either card 2 or card 3 must be a Three.) There is at least one Three just to the left of a Three. There is at least one Club just to the left of a Diamond, and there is at least one Club just to the right of a Club.

See if you can name the 3 cards.

When you know the answer, you can put the actual cards face down on a table and ask your friends if they can figure out what they are.

HOW CAN THIS BE?

Hold a pack of cards in your hand, and tell a friend the following story. A boy once dealt some cards to his three brothers. To the oldest he gave half the cards and half a card. He then gave half of the cards he had left and half a card to the second brother. Finally he gave half of the cards he then had left and half a card to his youngest brother. He then had no cards left.

At no time was a card cut, torn, or divided in any way. How many cards did he have at first? You proceed to show your friend by dealing out cards just as the boy did in the puzzle.

CARD PICKUP PUZZLE

Put 9 cards on the table arranged in 3 rows of 3 cards each, to form a square (Fig. 30). Then ask someone if he can pick up all the cards in 4 *continuous* straight lines. That is: He

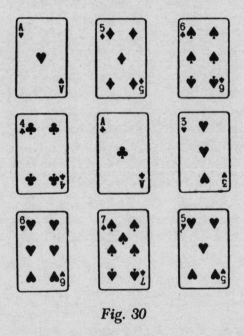

Fig. 30

must start at one card and pick up the line of cards of which it is the first one; the next line must start with a card next to the last card picked up, and the last two lines must start the same way. The lines may be straight across, up and down, or diagonal.

TURN OVER ALL BUT ONE

Put 10 cards face down on a table, arranged as shown in the drawing (Fig. 31). The puzzle then is to start at any face-down card counting it as 1, skip over 2 cards, counting clockwise, and turn the fourth card face up. You leave the card counted as 1 face down.

Fig. 31

You then pick another face-down card—any one—and do the same thing, turning the fourth card face up. Then continue until all the cards but one are face up.

You must always count a face-down card as 1 and land on a face-down card as the fourth card. If you don't know the secret, you will run out of face-down cards to use as the first and the fourth, before you reach the solution.

THE GIVE-AND-TAKE PUZZLE

A boy and a girl, Bill and Betty, each had a certain number of cards. Bill gave Betty as many cards as she already had.

When Betty received these cards, she asked Bill how many cards he had left, and promptly gave this number of cards back to Bill. Bill, not wishing to be greedy, gave Betty back as many cards as Betty had left. This left Bill without any cards and gave Betty 8 cards altogether. How many cards did each one have in the beginning?

ODD OR EVEN?

Give a friend a pack of cards and ask him to remove 2 piles—one containing an odd number of cards such as 3, 5 or 7, and the other containing an even number of cards such as 2, 4 or 6.

Ask him to hold 1 pile in his right hand and the other in his left hand, but not to let you know which hand holds which pile.

Now tell him to multiply the number of cards in his right hand by 3 and the number in his left hand by 2. Ask him to add these two products and to tell you whether the sum is an odd or even number. You can then tell him in which hand he is holding the odd number of cards and in which hand the even number.

THE TWENTY-FOUR CARD PUZZLE

This puzzle—or game—for it is both a puzzle and a game, is good for hours of fun. You can do it over and over again, each time in a different way, trying to get the best possible score for yourself, and you can also play against a friend who works the puzzle with a second pack of cards.

Put 24 cards on the table, arranged as in the drawing (Fig. 32). To start, pick up one of the cards two spaces from the center, like the one marked A, put it in the empty center space, and take out the card it "jumped" (B in the drawing).

Then jump any other card over another into an empty space and remove the card you jump each time.

The object is to remove as many cards as possible by jumping up, down, or across, but never jumping diagonally. If two people are playing, the winner is the one who has the fewest cards left when he can make no more jumps. If you can finish with only one card left, you are a marvel.

Fig. 32

SILLY SAM'S PACK OF CARDS

Silly Sam thought he would play cards one rainy afternoon, and decided to fix up an entirely new kind of pack. He made a pack of 33 cards, of which some were, naturally, red, and the others black.

In his pack there were 3 black to every 2 red cards among the plain cards; and 5 black to every 3 red cards among the face cards.

How many of each kind of card were there in the pack?

THE REVERSE-ORDER PUZZLE

This is one of the best of all card puzzles and, like "The Twenty-Four Card Puzzle," can be played a good deal like a game.

THE START

Fig. 33

Eleven cards, running from an Ace to a Jack, are arranged in 3 rows as shown in the drawing (Fig. 33). The puzzle then is to move the cards so as to reverse their order, ending up with the cards arranged as in the second drawing (Fig. 34).

THE FINISH

Fig. 34

The first move is to move either the Eight or the Jack into the empty space in the lower right-hand corner. Then move one card at a time into any space next to it. The cards may be moved straight across and up and down, but never diagonally.

The solution is given in the "Answers" section.

CARD LEAPFROG PUZZLE

Put 12 cards on the table, arranged as shown in the drawing (Fig. 35) in 3 rows of 4 cards each. Put an Ace at the left-hand end of the top row.

The puzzle now is to remove all the cards from the table

except the Ace, by jumping one card over the other as in checkers and removing the cards jumped over. At the end, the Ace is to be back in its original position.

Fig. 35

The circle with an X inside it is part of the puzzle and permits the first jump to be made. It is the only spot outside the puzzle, however, to which a card may be moved.

PUT-THEM-IN-ORDER PUZZLE

This is one of the classic "switching" puzzles, in which you have to move the cards about to rearrange them in a different order.

You start by putting on the table 6 cards; running from an Ace to a Six, arranged as shown in the drawing (Fig. 36). The puzzle is to shift the cards one at a time, until they are arranged in proper numerical order, with the Ace, Two and

Three in the top row, and the Four, Five and Six in the bottom row.

Fig. 36

The circle with an X inside it is part of the puzzle, for it is the only place to which the first move can be made. The cards are not jumped over one another. At each move a card is simply moved to an adjoining empty space.

ACE-TWO-THREE-FOUR PUZZLE

Take an Ace and a Two, Three and Four from the pack and put them face up in a pile on the table. Put the Four on the bottom of the pile, then the Three, then the Two, and the Ace on top.

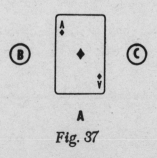

Fig. 37

Consider that the cards are on spot A, and that spots B and C are to the left and right, respectively, as in the drawing (Fig. 37). The puzzle is to move the cards one at a time so that finally they are all on spot C in the same order as they were on spot A. They can be moved to right or left, and over the cards in the middle, if necessary, but according to these rules:

1. A card may be moved only to an empty spot or
2. To a spot with a higher value card in the pile.
   The higher value card does not have to be the top card.
3. Make no more than 13 moves.

♠

Solutions to
PUZZLES WITH CARDS

♣

Solutions to Puzzles
with Cards

CHANGING THE ROWS

The solution is as follows:

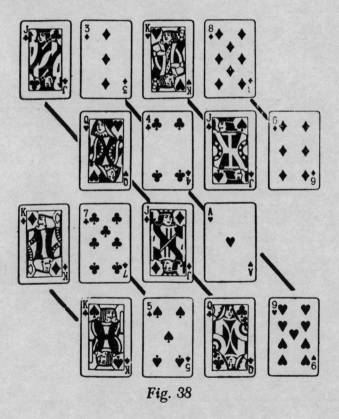

Fig. 38

Move the first left-hand card of the second row from the top over to the right, and do the same with the first left-hand card of the bottom row. Then count the two face cards at the lower left-hand corner as the first row, and so on. The catch is that the rows in the solution are on a slant.

THE ADD-TO-18 PUZZLE

Here is how you arrange the cards:

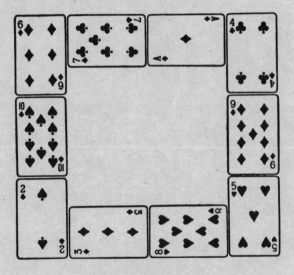

Fig. 39

THREE-IN-A-ROW

Move the card at the left over to the right end of the row. This changes the position of the original middle card and puts it—without touching it—at the left end of the row.

THE SIXTEEN-CARD PUZZLE

The cards are arranged as follows:

Jack of Diamonds—Queen of Clubs—King of Hearts—Ace of Spades.

King of Spades—Ace of Hearts—Jack of Clubs—Queen of Diamonds.

Ace of Clubs—King of Diamonds—Queen of Spades—Jack of Hearts.

Queen of Hearts—Jack of Spades—Ace of Diamonds—King of Clubs.

ALTERNATE CARDS

The four moves are shown below:

Fig. 40

THE FIVE-KINGS PUZZLE

Counting from the left, give each card a number, from 1 to 10 (Fig. 41). Put card number 4 on card number 1; then put 6 on 9; 8 on 3; 2 on 5; and 7 on 10.

Fig. 41

THE NOBLE LORDS AND THE COMMONERS

You need to touch with your hand only the center card in the top row. Pick it up and put it down again just beneath the center card in the bottom row. Then push up the entire middle column until the card you are touching becomes the center card of the bottom row.

TRICKY TRIANGLE

Give the cards numbers from top to bottom as shown in the drawing (Fig. 42). Move card 7 to the left of card 2; card 10 to the right of card 3; and card 1 to a point below and between cards 8 and 9.

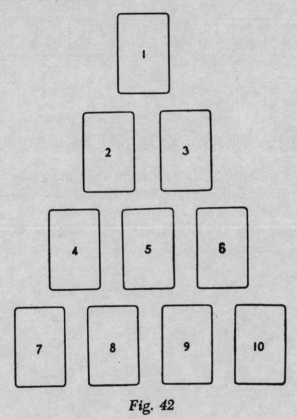

Fig. 42

FACE-UP

The cards are identified in the drawing below (Fig. 43) by the numbers 1, 2 and 3. The 3 moves are as follows. On the first move, turn over cards 2 and 3, turning card 2 face down and card 3 face up. On the second move, turn over

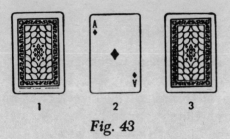

Fig. 43

cards 1 and 3. On the third and last move, turn over cards 2 and 3. All 3 cards will then be face up.

THE STAR PUZZLE

Here is the star:

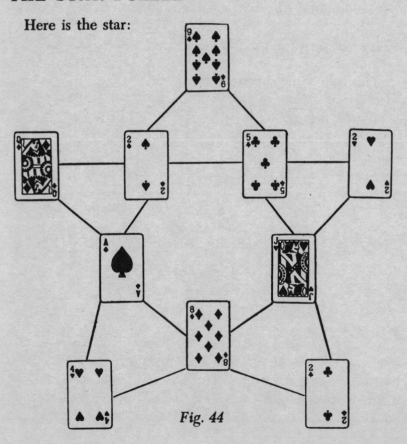

Fig. 44

THE JEALOUS KINGS

The King and Queen of Clubs go over first. The King of Clubs then returns alone.

The Queen of Hearts and the Queen of Diamonds go over. The Queen of Clubs returns by herself, and the King of Hearts and the King of Diamonds go over.

The King and Queen of Hearts return. The King of Clubs and the King of Hearts go over. The Queen of Diamonds returns alone.

The Queen of Clubs and the Queen of Hearts go over. The King of Diamonds then returns and takes over the Queen of Diamonds, and all of them are across the river.

THE HOURGLASS PUZZLE

This is how the cards are arranged:

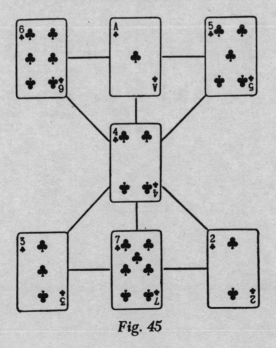

Fig. 45

THE EIGHTEEN-CARD CIRCLE

This is how you arrange the cards:

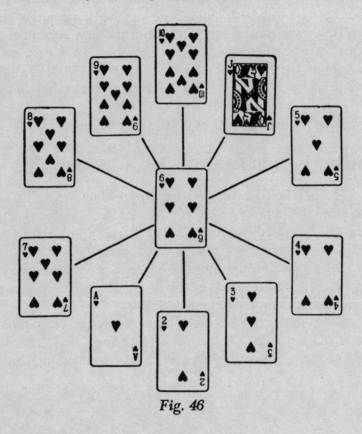

Fig. 46

A CARD BRAIN-TWISTER

The cards are:
1. The Two of Clubs
2. The Three of Clubs
3. The Three of Diamonds

The reasoning goes this way. There is at least one Three just to the right of a Two. That means that either card 2 or card 3 is a Three, because they are the only cards to the right of another card.

There is at least one Three just to the left of a Three. That means that either card 1 or card 2 is a Three. Since card 2 has been spotted both times as a Three, we know it is a Three.

Now, since card 2 is a Three and the first statement says that there is a Three just to the right of a Two, we are safe in assuming that card 1 is a Two. Then, since the second statement says that there is a Three (card 2) just to the left of a Three, we can guess that card 3 is a Three.

The suits are figured out in the same manner.

HOW CAN THIS BE?

The boy had 7 cards. When you are showing the solution to your friend, take 7 cards in your hand. You first deal half the cards and half a card. That is 3½ cards plus half a card, or 4. So you give your friend 4 cards, keeping 3.

The second brother got half of the cards left and half a card. This was 1½ cards plus half a card, or 2 and you give your friend 2 cards, keeping 1.

The youngest brother got half of the cards left and half a card. This was half a card plus half a card, or 1. You finish the solution by handing your friend the 1 remaining card.

CARD PICKUP PUZZLE

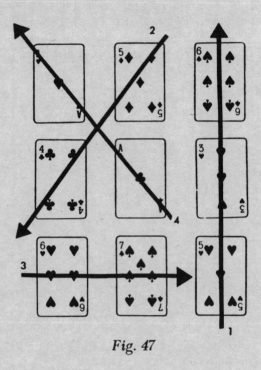

Fig. 47

The drawing shows the 4 continuous straight lines.

TURN OVER ALL BUT ONE

The solution of this puzzle is simple, and is easy to remember. It is this: Always arrange your starting point—each card number 1—so that you will turn face up the card that was the starting point of the preceding move.

The first card number 1 may be any card. It doesn't matter. But on your second move, make card number 1 the card 3 cards in a counter-clockwise direction away from the first card number 1. Then you will turn face up the first card number 1, which is in accordance with the formula given above

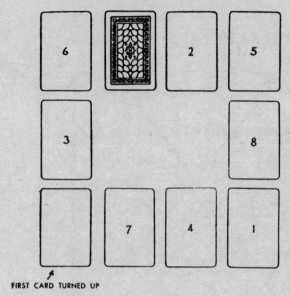

FIRST CARD TURNED UP

Fig. 48

This is such a good puzzle that I want to make it absolutely clear. The drawing (Fig. 48) should do this. It shows the cards you should start counting on, if you started with the card numbered 1. On the next move, start with card 2, on the next move with card 3, and so on.

THE GIVE-AND-TAKE PUZZLE

Bill had 5 cards, and Betty had 3. It is fun to take 5 cards yourself and give 3 to a friend and go through the different givings and takings to watch the puzzle work out.

ODD OR EVEN?

If the number he tells you is an even number, he is holding the even number of cards in his right hand. If it is an odd number, he is holding the odd number of cards in his right hand.

SILLY SAM'S PACK OF CARDS

There were 15 black and 10 red cards in the plain card part of the pack, and 5 black and 3 red cards in the face card part.

THE REVERSE-ORDER PUZZLE

The winning moves are as follows. Each card named is moved into a space that you will find empty next to it:

Jack, 10, 9, 5, 6, 7, 8.

Jack, 10, 9, 5, 6, Ace, 2, 3, 4.

Jack, 10, 9, 5, 6, Ace, 2, 3, 4.

Jack, 10, 9, 5, 6, Ace, 2, 3, 4.

Jack, 10, 9, 8, 6, Ace, 2, 3, 4.

Jack, 10, 9, 8, 5, Ace, 2, 3, 4.

7, 6, 5.

CARD LEAPFROG PUZZLE

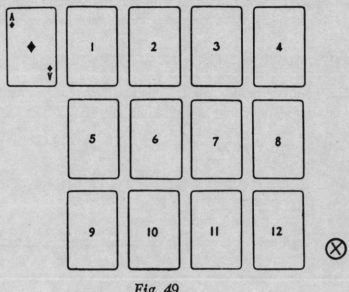

Fig. 49

The cards are numbered in this drawing (Fig. 49) so that you can follow the moves. These are as follows:

1. Jump 11 over 12 to X. Remove 12.
2. Jump 9 over 10 to 11. Remove 10.
3. Jump 2 over 6 to 10. Remove 6.
4. Jump 4 over 8 to 12. Remove 8.
5. Jump the Ace over 1 to 2, then over 3 to 4. Remove 1 and 3.
6. Jump 11 over 7 to 3. Remove 7.
7. Jump X over 12 to 11, then over 10 to 9, then over 5 to 1. Remove 12, 10 and 5.
8. Jump 4 (the Ace) over 3 to 2, and then over 1 to its original position. Remove 3 and 1.

PUT-THEM-IN-ORDER PUZZLE

Fig. 50

On each move there will be only one space open to which
a card can be shifted. Move the cards in the following order:
Two to X, Four, Three, Six, Four, Three, Five, Ace, Three,
Four, Six, Five, Four, Three, Ace, Four, Five, Six, Three, Two.

ACE-TWO-THREE-FOUR PUZZLE

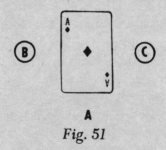

Fig. 51

The moves are made as follows; reading down:

Ace to B	Ace to B	Two to A	Ace to B
Two to C	Two to B	Ace to A	Two to C
Ace to C	Four to C	Three to C	Ace to C
Three to B			

♥

20 SOLITAIRES

♠

20 Solitaires

Solitaire games, or Patience games, as they are sometimes called, are wonderful fun at any time. They can be played by one person, and offer a grand way to amuse yourself on trains, on rainy afternoons or evenings, or whenever time is passing slowly. Good solitaires can make the hours fly.

Almost everybody knows how to play Canfield and Klondike, the first two solitaires described in this section; and many people know one or two others. What I hope you will do is to learn four or five of the ones you like the best. Then you will have a way to keep yourself amused and entertained for hours, wherever you are. Solitaires are one of the very best answers to the question, "What shall I do now?"

CANFIELD

This solitaire is said to have been invented by Richard A. Canfield, a famous New York cardplayer. Some people know Canfield as Klondike, and there is another very good solitaire called Klondike, which often goes under the name of Canfield. No one seems to know how this mix-up in names came about. However, by whichever name you call them, you are sure to enjoy both games.

This is how you play Canfield:

1. Shuffle the cards. Count off 13 cards face down into a pile. Turn the pile up and put it on your left. This is your 13 pile, or stock pile.

2. Deal the next, or fourteenth, card face up. Put it out

[77]

in the middle of the table, since it is to be a foundation card
on which other cards will be played (Fig. 1). Suppose this
card is a Five. The other 3 Fives, when you come to them,
will then be the other foundation cards. The object of the
game is to play as many cards as possible onto these foundation cards.

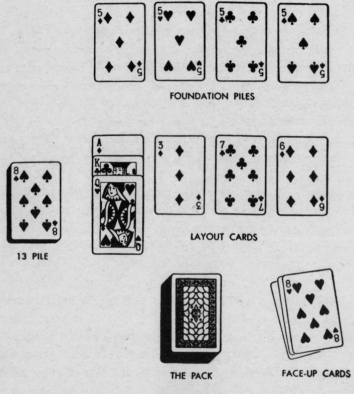

Fig. 1

3. Put the next 4 cards face up in a row between yourself
and the foundation card, as in Fig. 1. We shall call these 4
cards the layout cards.

Now you are ready to play, and this is what you do:

1. Count off 3 cards in a single group, from the top of the
pack remaining in your hand. Put them on the table, all face

up in a pile. In this way, the third card from the top of the pack becomes the top card of the face-up pile. If you can play this card onto a foundation card or onto one of the 4 layout cards, do so, in this way: On the foundation cards, always *build up*, using cards of the same suit as the foundation card. If a foundation card is the Five of Hearts, for example, the next card that goes on it is the Six of Hearts, then, as the game goes on, the Seven of Hearts, and so on. Keep on building up to the King, then go right on with the Ace, Two, Three, and other higher cards until you have played all 13 cards of the suit—if you can. On the 4 layout cards, *build down*, and *alternate* (take turns with) the cards according to color—a red Eight on a black Nine, then a black Seven on the red Eight, a red Six on the black Seven, and so forth. When you get an Ace at the bottom of a column of cards, you can keep right on building down. Put a King on the Ace, a Queen on the King, and so on.

2. *The 13 Pile.* Whenever you can, move the top card of the 13 pile to one of the foundation piles or to one of the columns building down from the layout cards. *Do not build up or down on the 13 pile.* Just get rid of its cards as fast as you can.

3. Continue playing by counting off 3 cards at a time from the pack in your hand and playing the third card if possible. If you play it, you may also be able to play the card under it, and the next cards too, if there are places to put them.

4. You can move onto the foundation piles the top cards from the 13 pile, the layout cards, or the face-up cards dealt out from the pack. Always watch for a chance to do so.

5. While you are playing, you can move cards from one column to another of the layout cards, but they must always build down on a column to which they are moved, and a whole sequence must always be moved at once. A sequence in Canfield is 2 or more cards in a column, each one number lower than the one on which it rests, such as an Eight with a Seven and Six built down on it. If there is a single card in a

column and you move it, it must build *down* on the column
to which you move it. For example, you can take a black
Eight and put it on a red Nine in another column. But if cards
have been built down on the black Eight to form a sequence,
you must move them too, along with the Eight. Watch for a
chance to do this, since by moving sequences whenever possible, you may make space to put out more cards.

6. If you play or move all the cards in one column, leaving
an empty space, you can fill the space *only* with a card from
the 13 pile, as long as there are cards in that pile. When the
13 pile is used up, you can fill a space with the top card of
the face-up cards on the table.

7. Continue until all the cards in your hand have been
dealt face up in a pile on the table. Then turn them face down
and deal them off again in groups of 3. Do not shuffle or cut
the cards. Keep on until you have either won the game by
getting all the cards onto the foundation piles, or can't play
any more cards. Then count the cards in the foundation piles
to get your score.

Many players follow the rule that cards on top of the four
foundation piles may be played back into the four layout
columns of cards, whenever they can be used in building a
sequence. This is a good variation that adds interest.

Some people play that the cards may be dealt out from the
pack in your hand only three times, after which the game
ends. Others turn up the cards 1 at a time instead of in groups
of 3, and go through the pack only once. There is no strict
rule. You can play whichever way you want to.

KLONDIKE

As I mentioned before, this is the solitaire that many people
call Canfield. This is the way you play:

1. To arrange the cards for Klondike, shuffle the pack, and
then deal the top card of the pack face up on the table. Deal
the next 6 cards in a row to the right of it, putting them face

down. Deal the next card face up on the first face-down card. Deal the next 5 cards face down in a row to the right, partly covering the 5 other face-down cards. Continue in the same way until the cards are arranged as in Fig. 2.

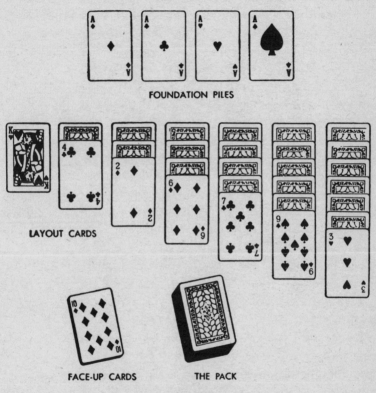

Fig. 2

2. Then deal cards 3 at a time from the pack in your hand, putting them face up on the table. Thus, on the first deal, the third card from the top will be face up on top of the dealt cards.

The original foundation cards in Klondike are the Aces. Whenever an Ace turns up, you put it out in front of the other cards. Then you try to build up on the Aces, always adding cards of the same suit only—the Two of Diamonds on the Ace of Diamonds, the Two of Clubs on the Ace of Clubs, and so on. The object of the game is to build from Ace to King on the foundation cards of each suit.

3. Cards may be moved from the face-up cards dealt onto the table from the pack in your hand to the columns of layout cards when they build *down* in sequence and are opposite in color to the card on which they are placed. A red Seven goes on a black Eight, and so on.

4. Cards may be moved onto the foundation cards, either from the uppermost of the columns of the layout cards, or from the top of the pile of cards dealt from your hand.

5. Cards and sequences of cards may be moved from one column of the layout cards to another, always building down and being opposite in color. Whole sequences *must* be moved together. You may not move part of a sequence.

6. When you move a card or a sequence of cards from a column and leave the bottom face-down card of the column uncovered, turn this card face up immediately and see if you can play it or move other cards onto it to build down.

7. When you use up an entire column of cards and have an empty space, you can fill the space *only* with a King. After all 4 Kings have filled spaces, however, you can use any face-up card, either from the dealt-out cards or from a column, if the card is not part of a sequence. You can even move a sequence of cards from a column to fill an empty space. There is no rule against it. In fact, it is a good idea, since in this way you may uncover a face-down card which you can use.

8. Continue dealing out your pack 3 at a time, without shuffling. When you have gone through the pack, pick it up and deal it again.

The game ends either when all 52 cards have been played onto the foundation piles or when you can't move any more cards. If you wish, you may limit the number of times you can deal out the pack in your hand. A common rule is that the pack can be dealt out only three times. Others deal the cards one at a time, and go through the pack only once.

ELEVENS

This is a fairly easy solitaire to win. It will probably work out for you four out of every five times you play it.

Shuffle the pack well and then deal out 12 cards, face up, in 3 rows of 4 cards each. If you deal a Jack, a Queen or a King, pick it up from the table and put it on the bottom of the pack. Deal the next card out on the table in its place.

When the 12 cards have been dealt, look for any 2 of them that total 11, such as a Ten and an Ace (which counts as 1 in this game), a Nine and a Two, an Eight and a Three, and so on. When you find 2 such cards, cover each of them with a card dealt face up from the pack in your hand. Whenever you come to a Jack, Queen or King, put it on the bottom of the pack, and deal another card to cover one of the "elevens" cards.

Continue covering pairs of cards that add up to 11 as long as you can. If you can keep this up until you come to the court cards—the Jacks, Queens and Kings—you have put on the bottom of the pack, you win the game. Deal out the 12 court cards, one on top of each pile. This shows that you have won.

PERPETUAL MOTION

Perpetual Motion keeps you busy, moving one card right after the other, until you either win or lose. In this solitaire, you move cards, instead of building them up and down.

Shuffle and deal out all the cards in the pack, *face up*, into 13 piles of 4 cards each. Arrange the piles in 2 rows, with 7 piles in the top row, and 6 piles in the bottom row, as in Fig. 3. The piles represent the cards in order, from Ace to King. The Aces represent 1, the Jacks represent 11, the Queens 12, and the Kings 13.

Look at the top card, face up on pile 1. If it is an Ace, leave it there and go to the second pile. If the top card on pile 1 is not an Ace, put it, *face up*, at the bottom of pile 2. Then put the top card of pile 2, face up, under pile 3; the top card of pile 3, face up, under pile 4, and so on, unless you come to a pile of which the top card has the same value as the pile. In that case, skip over it without touching it. If the top card of pile 8, for example, is an Eight, skip the pile. Put the top card of pile 7 under pile 9, and put its top card in turn face up under pile 10.

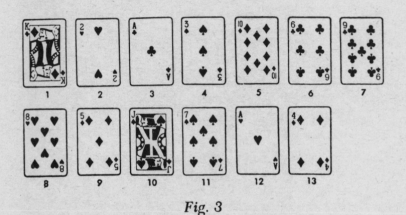

Fig. 3

Move the top card of pile 13 to the bottom of pile 1, unless pile 1 has an Ace on top of it. If this is the case, put the top card of pile 13 under pile 2 or the first pile of which the top card is not of the same value as the pile.

When the top cards of all 13 piles have the same values as the piles, remove these top 13 cards and put them to one side as a completed set or sequence. Begin the next set with the pile where the first set was completed. For example, if the last pile under which you put a card was pile 6, remove the top card of pile 6 and put it under pile 7.

If you can complete and put to one side 3 sets of 13 cards running from the Ace to the King, you win the game. Sometimes you get blocked before you can finish the first set. If this happens, shuffle the cards and start over again.

EVEN UP

Even Up is an easy solitaire. This is how it is played:

Take the Jacks, Queens, and Kings from the pack and put them to one side. Shuffle the remaining cards. Then hold the pack face down in your hand and deal 1 card face up on the table.

Deal a second card. If the total of the second card and the first card is an even number, pick up both cards and put them aside. For example, the first card might be a Five and the second card a Three. Their total would be 8—an even number —so they are picked up and put to one side.

The object of the game is to put aside in pairs all the cards that total even numbers. The Ace counts as 1.

If you deal a card and a second card, and their total is an odd number, leave both cards on the table, face up, with the second card on top of the first. Deal a third card and see if it, added to the second card, the top one, makes an even number. If it does not, put it on top of the second card, deal a fourth card and see if it makes an even number when added to the third card. On each play, you count only 2 cards—the one on top of the pile on the table, and the one just dealt from the hand.

You are allowed to go through the pack only once.

BEEHIVE

This is a good and little-known solitaire. When the cards come off the pack just right, you can win very easily. But many a game gets blocked just when you least expect it.

Shuffle the pack. Then, holding the cards face down, count off 10 cards and put them in a pile face up on the table, with only the top card showing. This is the beehive.

Deal off the next 6 cards, placing them in 2 horizontal rows of 3 cards each. This is the flower garden into which you try to get the bees, or cards in the beehive, as well as all the other

cards. Hold the remainder of the pack in your hand, face
down.

The object is to combine all the 52 cards in sets of 4 of a
kind, such as 4 Twos, 4 Fives, and so on, by grouping them
in sets of 4 in the flower garden, and removing each set when
it is completed.

With the cards laid out as described (Fig. 4), begin to
send the bees to the garden. If the top card of the beehive is
the same in value as any card in the garden, place it on that
card. Then the next card in the hive, being uncovered, may
be used if it has the same value as any card in the garden.

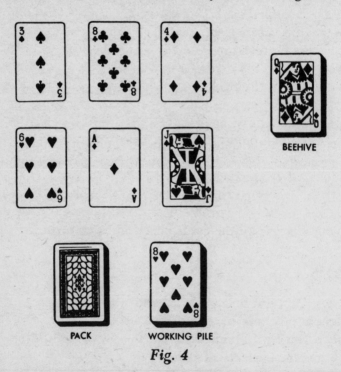

Fig. 4

No card is ever placed on the beehive, since the object is
to use up all its cards as quickly as possible. Cards are placed
only on the 6 garden cards.

If 2 cards in the garden have the same value, place one

on top of the other, and fill the vacant space with the top card of the beehive.

When all the cards of the same value, among the cards on the table, have been combined, deal off 3 cards from the pack in your hand, placing them in a pile face up, with only the top card (the third card from the top of the pack) showing. This will begin a working pile. If the top card has the same value as any card in the garden, place it on the garden card, and use the card it uncovers in the working pile if it, too, has the same value as any in the garden.

When you complete a set of 4 cards of the same value in the garden, such as 4 Threes, remove it, put it to one side, and fill the vacant space with the top card of the beehive. When there are no more cards in the beehive, fill a vacant space with the top card of the working pile.

Go through the pack 3 cards at a time, placing them face up on the working pile and using as many as you can on cards in the garden, building sets of 4. Then turn over the working pile and go through it again, 3 cards at a time. It may be turned over and gone through as many times as you wish, but it must not be shuffled.

If you finally go through the working pile without being able to use a single card that is turned up, you lose the game. If you combine all the cards in sets of 4, you win.

GAPS

Gaps requires a large table, because you have to lay all 52 cards out, one by one. This is a tight fit for most card tables. You can, if you wish, lay the cards out on the floor, where there is plenty of room.

Shuffle the pack well and then deal all the cards, face up, one at a time, in 4 horizontal rows of 13 cards each. Pick up the 4 Aces and put them to one side, and there will be 4 gaps or empty spaces in the layout. The object of the game is to move cards, filling the gaps, so that the Twos will all be in the first spaces at the left end of the rows, and the rows will all be built up in sequence and in the same suit from the Twos to the Kings. One row will be all Hearts, for example, another one will be all Spades, and so on. And the cards in each row are to run in order from left to right, starting with the Two and ending with the King.

When moving cards to fill gaps, you must always build up, putting a card of the next higher value, and of the same suit, to the right of a card already in position. Move the Seven of Clubs to the right of the Six of Clubs, for example; but never move the Six of Clubs (a card of lower value) to the left of the Seven of Clubs. And no card may be put in a gap to the right of a King.

Whenever the first space at the left of a row becomes vacant, it is to be filled with a Two.

Move all the cards you can and then, as a rule, you will find that you are blocked, and cannot move any more. When you get blocked, pick up all the cards that do not form part of a sequence beginning with a Two that is properly placed at the left of a row. Shuffle the cards and deal them out again. Leave one gap after each of the sequences that remains on the table. If there is a row with no sequence beginning with a Two, leave the first space open for a Two.

Strict players allow themselves only one extra deal. But most people allow themselves 3 extra deals and I have found it more fun to play Gaps that way.

ROLL CALL or TALKATIVE

Roll Call is a game in which you have to talk as well as deal out cards. It is also known as Talkative. This is how you play:

Shuffle the cards. Hold the pack in your hand and deal the cards onto the table, one at a time, into a pile, face up. As you deal, count out loud "Ace, Two, Three, Four," and so on up to "Ten, Jack, Queen, King." Whenever a card dealt has the same value as your count, it answers the roll call. You put that card to one side. For example, suppose you count "Ace, Two, Three, Four, Five" and as you say "Five," you deal a Five. You put the Five to one side.

When you have dealt all the cards, pick up the ones that didn't answer the roll call, and deal them again, counting as you do so. Start counting, with the top card, from where you just left off. If the last card dealt was counted 6, call the top card dealt right after it 7.

The object of the game is to get all the cards to answer to their names, and so move all of them from the pack to one side. Some players deal the pack 3 times and then add up the cards removed to get their score. Others continue dealing and try to get all the cards to answer the roll call, going through the pack as few times as possible.

IDLE YEAR

Idle Year is a good name for this solitaire. It is easy to play and you can take all the time you want. The moves are simple and interesting.

Use a full pack, shuffle the cards, and start by dealing them, one at a time, in a row. Watch out for any 2 cards that are of the same suit, such as 2 Hearts, or 2 cards that are of the same value, such as 2 Sevens.

If 2 cards of the same suit or the same value are dealt next to each other, move the second or right-hand one onto the first. For example, if you deal a Three of Hearts and then a Five of Hearts, put the Five on top of the Three. Or if you deal a Ten and then another Ten right beside it, put the second Ten on the first.

Furthermore, if 2 cards of the same suit or of the same value have 2 cards between them, move the second card of the same suit or value to the left, over the 2 in-between cards, and put it on the first.

Watch for opportunities to make 2 or more moves in a row. You might, for example, move a Ten of Hearts onto a Five

of Hearts to its left. There might then be another Ten just
beyond the 2 cards, to the left of the Ten of Hearts. You could
then move the Ten of Hearts and Five of Hearts onto the
other Ten.

If a card to be moved already has other cards beneath it,
you move the whole pile.

Sometimes you have a choice of putting a card on the card
directly to its left or of jumping it to the left over 2 inter-
vening cards. There is no way, in this game, to know which is
the better move. You must make a choice and then stick to it.

The object of the game is to move all the cards in the pack
onto the first card dealt.

ROUND THE CLOCK

This is an old favorite solitaire with many people. Luck
counts a great deal, for the way the cards fall when you deal
them determines how close you can come to winning. There
is a good deal of fun, and even excitement, however, in trying
to work the game out to a successful conclusion.

After shuffling the cards, start by dealing in a circle 12 piles
of 4 cards each, all face down, and another pile of 4 cards
face down in the center of the circle (Fig. 5). The 12 piles
represent the figures on the face of a clock, and they also
represent the numbers of the cards from the Ace (1), Two,
Three up to the Jack (11) and the Queen (12). The 4 cards
in the center form the King pile.

Now try to get all the cards in their correct places, face
up, before the King pile is completed—the 4 Aces in pile 1,
the 4 Twos in pile 2, the 4 Threes at three o'clock, and so on.
Start with pile 1 (the Ace pile). Turn over the top card and
put it, face up, at the bottom of its correct pile. If it is a Six,
for example, put it face up beneath pile 6. Then turn over the
top card of pile 6 and put it beneath its correct pile. If it is a
Ten, put it beneath pile 10, and so on. Whenever you turn
up a King, it goes face up beneath the center pile.

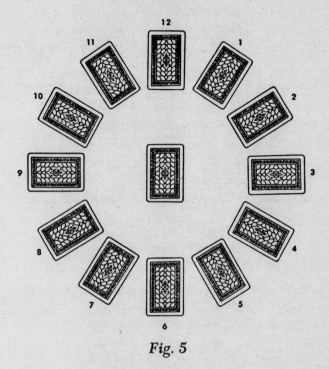

Fig. 5

If you succeed in winning, you will have all the cards in their correct positions, from the 4 Aces at one o'clock to the 4 Queens at twelve o'clock. But if the 4 Kings are turned up before you complete the other piles, the game comes to an end right then and there.

PIRATE GOLD

This is one of the easiest of all solitaires to play—and to win; so if you want to while away some time and have the fun of winning, play a few games and get some of the Pirate Gold.

To start the game, shuffle the cards and deal 5 of them onto the table, face up in a row. Beneath them on the table deal another row of 5 face-up cards, as in Fig. 6.

Fig. 6

These cards are called the "pirate's goldpieces." The object of the game is to put other cards on top of them to make piles of gold pieces.

This is how you play:

Look at the 10 cards on the table and see if any 2 of them have the same value and make a pair, such as 2 Fours, 2 Sevens, or 2 Queens.

If there is a pair of 2 like cards, cover each of the 2 cards with a card dealt face up from the pack in your hand. If there is more than 1 pair, cover all the pairs.

The new cards you have added will usually make some new pairs. Cover these by dealing cards from the pack. Then keep on covering pairs and see if you can deal out all the cards in the pack.

If you succeed in doing this, you win the game. But if you get "stuck" by reaching a point when there are no pairs on the table to cover, you lose that game.

It sometimes happens, though not very often, that there are no pairs among the first 10 cards you put on the table. When this occurs, pick up the cards, shuffle them, and deal out 10 new cards.

LAZY BOY

This is another of the easier solitaires. You will probably be able to win it several times in a row every time you play it. But you have to watch the cards carefully as you turn them up, and not get caught napping.

Shuffle the cards and hold the pack in your hand face down. Start by dealing off the 3 top cards and putting them face up on the table, with the third card from the top on top. If this card is an Ace or a King, put it in the center of the table to build on. All the Aces and Kings are put in the center of the table side by side as you come to them in going through the pack.

On the Aces you build up to the Sevens of the same suit, always playing cards of that suit. For example, on the Ace of Hearts, you put the Two, Three, Four, Five, Six and Seven of Hearts. On the Kings you build down to the Eights of the same suit. On the King of Spades, for example, you would put the Queen, Jack, Ten, Nine and Eight of Spades.

Suppose that the first card you turn up (the third card from the top of the pack) is an Ace or a King. Put it in the center of the table. Then suppose that the card beneath it is a Two or a Queen and can be played. You play it also right away, and the card beneath it, if it too can be played.

After you have done all you can with the first 3 cards, you deal off 3 more, putting them face up on top of the others. Play the top card if you can, and any cards beneath it. Then deal off 3 more cards and place them face up on the pile.

Go right through the pack in this way, dealing 3 cards at a time, putting all the Aces and Kings in the center of the table, and building up on the Aces and down on the Kings.

When you have gone through the pack once, turn it over, and without shuffling the cards, go through it again, and play every face-up card you can.

Continue turning the cards over, after each time you go through them, and try to play out all the cards onto the center piles. If you can do this, you win the game. If you cannot complete the building up and down on the center piles, you lose the game.

AULD LANG SYNE

Auld Lang Syne is an old favorite, and it is one of the easiest of the solitaires.

Start by shuffling the cards and putting the 4 Aces on the table in a row. Then deal the first 4 cards on top of the pack in a row beneath them, as in Fig. 7.

Fig. 7

The object of the game is to build up on the 4 Aces, according to suit. All the Hearts go on the Ace of Hearts, all the Spades on the Ace of Spades, and so on.

If there are any Twos in the first 4 cards you put on the table, you can play them on the Aces right away.

If there are no Twos, deal 4 more cards on top of the first 4. Play some of these and some of those under them, if possible.

Keep on dealing in this way until you have gone through the pack. Then pick up the 4 piles for another deal, putting the right-hand pile on top of the one to its left. Put these 2 piles on the one to the left, and the 3 piles on the left-hand pile. Then, according to the general rule, you can go through the pack two times more—or three times in all.

By that time you should have a lot of cards built up on the Aces, or you may even have won the game, for Auld Lang Syne gives you a good chance to win.

GRANDFATHER'S CLOCK

Grandfather's Clock has been a favorite for many years.

You start by putting face up on the table 12 cards—a Two, Three, Four, Five, Six, Seven, Eight, Nine, Ten, Jack, Queen and King. These are arranged in the form of a clock dial but with the Two in the position of the 5 o'clock hand, as in Fig. 8.

The first card—the Two—may be of any suit, but it must be followed by 3 cards of 3 other suits. Look at Fig. 8 and you will see that the Two of Hearts is followed (going clockwise) by the Three of Clubs, the Four of Diamonds and the Five of Spades. The order of the suits that you use for the first 4 cards must be used with each of the other two 4-card sequences.

When you have made the clock dial, deal out the remaining 40 cards of the pack face up into 8 piles of 5 cards each. Put these in front of you below the clock. All the cards in the piles are face up.

The object of the game is to move cards from the 8 piles at the bottom onto the cards in the circle to make the circle represent the numbers on a clock dial. You have to build up the piles in the circle by adding cards of the same suit. Thus, only the Three of Hearts can go on the Two of Hearts. Then the Four of Hearts goes on the Three, and so on. On the Ten, Jack, Queen and King, you build up to the Ace (1), then the Two, Three and Four.

If you are able to play all the cards, the top cards of the piles in the circle will represent the numbers of a clock dial and will all be in the same places as on a clock.

Fig. 8

Here are the simple rules you must follow:

The top cards of the eight piles are played onto the piles in the circle, building up in numerical sequence and suit. This has already been explained in describing the object of the game.

The top cards of the 8 piles may be built down on each other, without regard to color. Thus, you can put either a red or a black Six on a black Seven, a red or a black Two on a red Three, and so on. The colors do not have to alternate. Just let each card be one lower in value than the card you put it on.

When the top card of one of the 8 piles is removed, the card underneath it becomes the top card and may be played onto another one of the 8 piles or onto a pile in the circle.

The game ends either when all the cards are on the piles in the circle or when you can't move any more cards.

IDIOT'S DELIGHT

This name has been given to a number of solitaire games, but this is the one usually called Idiot's Delight.

The cards are arranged for the game by dealing out 45 of them face up as shown in Fig. 9. The first 9 cards go in the top row, the next 8 in the second overlapping row, the next 7 in the third overlapping row, and so on. This will make 9 columns of cards, of varying lengths.

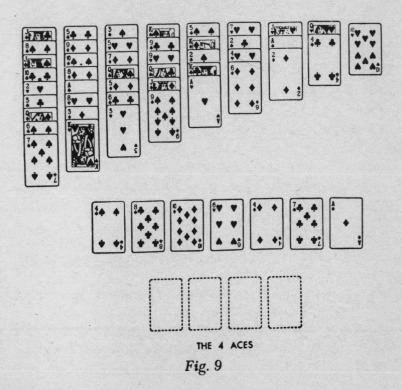

THE 4 ACES

Fig. 9

You will have 7 cards left, and these are laid out face up in a row, below the other cards.

As you play, you will put the 4 Aces below these 7 cards, and will build up on them. The 4 Aces are the bottom cards of the foundation piles. Be sure, therefore, to leave enough room on the table for these piles, which are indicated in Fig. 9 by the 4 cards with dotted outlines.

The object of the game is to build up as many cards as possible on top of the 4 Aces. All the cards in each of these foundation piles must be of the same suit.

The rules of Idiot's Delight are as follows:

Uncovered cards in the 9 columns may be played on each other. In these columns, build down and alternate the colors of the cards, putting a red Three on a black Four, a black Ten on a red Jack, and so on. *You may move only one card at any one time. You are not allowed to move sequences.*

Whenever you uncover an Ace, by moving another card from on top of it, put it below the 7 cards, so that you can start building up on it.

Build up on the Aces in sequence and by suit. That is, put the Two of Clubs on the Ace of Clubs, the Two of Hearts on the Ace of Hearts, and so on up to the King.

Uncovered cards in the columns may be moved onto a foundation pile.

Any of the 7 cards below the columns may be moved to a foundation pile; played on a card in one of the columns, building down and alternating colors; or used to fill an empty space among the columns.

Empty spaces in the 9 columns may be filled by any uncovered card. You do not have to use a King, for example, as in some other solitaires.

You are not allowed to build on the 7 cards, and you are not allowed to fill the spaces made by removing these cards.

The game ends when you have won by putting all the cards on the 4 foundation piles or when no more cards can be moved.

STREETS AND ALLEYS

Streets and Alleys is a fairly widely-known solitaire, which should be even more popular. It is played on the same principle as most other solitaires, but some people like it better because you can build cards on each other regardless of their suits.

After shuffling, the cards are dealt face up onto the table as shown in Fig. 10. There are 4 horizontal rows of 7 cards each on the left, and 4 horizontal rows of 6 cards each on the right. The Main Street runs up the center, and the alleys run off to the right and left between the rows of cards.

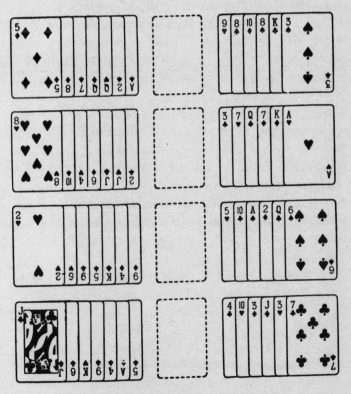

Fig. 10

The 4 Aces are to be placed in the Main Street as soon as you can uncover them, and their final positions are shown by the cards with the dotted outlines (Fig. 10).

The object of the game is to get the Aces out into the Main Street and then to build up on them the remaining cards of their suits—or as many of the remaining cards as possible. Build up by suits—the Two, Three, Four of Hearts and the remaining Hearts on the Ace of Hearts, and the same for the three other suits.

The rules of Streets and Alleys are as follows:

You may move only the outside cards, on the ends of the rows away from the Main Street.

You may move only one card at a time and it must build *down* on another outside end card. Cards can be put beside other cards regardless of color or suit. The only thing that counts is the number or value of the cards. Thus, in Fig. 10, you can move the Seven of Clubs over to the Eight of Hearts. Then you can move the Six of Spades to the Seven of Clubs, following by moving the Five of Diamonds to the Six of Spades. Next you can move the Two of Hearts over to the Three of Spades.

You may not move sequences—only single cards.

When you move an end card, the card next to it becomes an end card and can be played.

When you move away all the cards in any row and leave a space, you may fill the space with any end card you wish to move.

Whenever an Ace becomes an end card, move it into the Main Street and build up on it with cards of the same suit, when they become end cards.

You win the game when you get all the cards out and onto the 4 piles in the Main Street. Sometimes you get "stuck" before that point and cannot move any more cards.

ROYAL MARRIAGE

Here is a first-rate solitaire in which you don't build down or up, as in most others. It works on an entirely different plan, and one that makes you keep your eyes open, watching the cards.

Start by shuffling the pack of cards, and then putting the King of Hearts on the bottom and the Queen of Hearts on the top. The object of the game is to bring these two widely-separated monarchs together at the very end.

Put the Queen of Hearts on the table face up, and deal the 4 next cards in a row face up to her right, as in Fig. 11.

Fig. 11

Now see if you can discard any card or cards by the following procedure: If there are 2 cards of the same suit in the row, but separated by either 1 or 2 cards, pick up the "in-between" card or cards and discard them—not to be used any more. Then move the card on the right over beside the card of the same suit to the left.

Look at Fig. 11 to see how this works. You discard the Five of Spades, which separates 2 cards of the same suit—Hearts. Then you discard the Two of Clubs, which separates 2 cards of the same suit, the Queen of Hearts and the Four of Hearts. Then you move the Four of Hearts and Two of Hearts over to the left, and have Fig. 11-A. Here again the Queen of Hearts and Two of Hearts are separated by a card. This card happens to be of the same suit—the Four of Hearts —but out it goes. You discard it and have the Queen and the Two of Hearts left. Move the Two to the left so that it is be-

Fig. 11-A

side the Queen. Fig. 11 shows cards of the same suit separated by only 1 other card. But if 2 other cards are side by side between 2 cards of the same suit, you may discard both of the "in-between" cards.

Follow the same procedure when 2 cards of the same *value* appear in the row of 4 cards to the right of the Queen. If these cards are separated by 1 or 2 other cards, discard the card or cards between them, and move the card at the right over to the left.

After doing what you can with the first 4 cards dealt out, deal out 4 more cards, placing them in the same positions as the first 4 cards. Some of these will cover cards already on the table—left over from the first deal.

After the second deal, you will probably have one or more *piles* of cards, owing to the fact that you have dealt cards on top of other cards. These piles are discarded just as though each were a single card, when the top card of the pile is one that is to be discarded. There is sometimes a choice of two plays, but in this game there is no way of knowing which will be the best, since your chances of winning depend upon what succeeding cards are dealt out.

Continue dealing out 4 cards at a time until you come to the bottom of the pack. Then, if you are lucky, you may be able to bring the Queen and King together.

HIDDEN CARDS

This is quite a hard solitaire to win. You can, however, figure your score for each game and so, even though you do not win, can count each game as a good one or an unlucky one. The score is the total number of piles of 4 cards that you succeed in turning face up, counting each pile as 1.

Shuffle the pack and deal it, 1 card at a time, face down, into 12 piles of 4 cards each, making 3 horizontal rows, each containing 4 piles. The remaining 4 cards are put in a 13 pile below the other cards, also face down, to be drawn from when needed (Fig. 12).

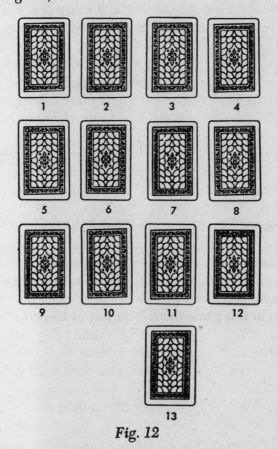

Fig. 12

The object of the game is to move the cards, as described below, so that all the Aces are in the first pile, the Twos in the second pile, and so on.

In this game, the Aces count as 1, the Jacks as 11, the Queens as 12, and all the other cards according to the number of their spots. The Kings are discarded as they appear during the playing.

Start by turning over the top card of the 13 pile, and playing it, face up, under the pile that corresponds to its value. For example, if it is a Nine, place it under the pile numbered 9 in the illustration. Then turn up the top card of the 9 pile and place it, face up, under the pile that corresponds to its value. Keep repeating this process until a King appears. Discard the King and start over again with the next card from the 13 pile.

If the 13 pile is used up, or if the 4 Kings appear before all the cards in all the piles are turned face up, the game is lost.

FIFTEENS

In Fifteens the object is to combine 2 or more cards *of the same suit* whose values total 15 and to discard them; and to keep on making as many as possible "fifteens" in this way. If you can combine and discard all 52 cards, you win the game.

Shuffle and deal out 16 cards in 4 rows of 4 cards each face up, as in Fig. 13. Keep the rest of the pack to deal from as you have spaces to fill.

There are only two things you have to remember. These are:

1. You may combine any 2 or more cards (even 3 or 4 or 5 cards) to make "fifteens." But these cards must be of the *same suit*.

2. In addition, if a Ten, Jack, Queen and King of the *same suit* are on the table at any one time, you can pick up all 4 of them and discard them. This does not happen very often and at other times the Tens, Jacks, Queens and Kings are combined with other cards. The Aces count 1, the Jacks count 11, the Queens 12, and the Kings 13.

Fig. 13

Now, let's look at Fig. 13 and see what can be done. First you can combine the Three, Four and Eight of Hearts to make 15, and put them to one side.

Next, you can pick up the Ten, Jack, Queen and King of Diamonds, according to Rule 2, and can put them out of the game.

You then have 7 empty spaces. Fill them with cards dealt from the pack in your hand, and see if you can make any more "Fifteens."

The game continues until you win it by combining and discarding all the cards, or until you get stuck and can't make any more combinations.

TEN OF CLUBS

This is a famous and exciting solitaire, in which your success is governed entirely by chance. The game ends when you turn up the Ten of Clubs, and it may be the first card—or the last.

The game is played with 20 cards only. These are the Ten, Jack, Queen, King and Ace of each suit.

Remove these cards from the pack, shuffle them well, and lay them out face down as shown in Fig. 14. The first 3 rows contain 5 cards each, and the bottom row contains 4 cards. The last card is kept in your hand.

Fig. 14

Start by looking at the card in your hand. Suppose it is the Ten of Diamonds. Place it where the Ten of Diamonds is meant to go, according to the following arrangement of the cards:

Top Row   —Ace, King, Queen, Jack, Ten of Spades

2nd Row   —Ace, King, Queen, Jack, Ten of Hearts

3rd Row   —Ace, King, Queen, Jack, Ten of Diamonds

Bottom Row—Ace, King, Queen, Jack, Ten of Clubs

Put the Ten of Diamonds at the right end of the third row face up. Then turn face up the card that was there in the first place. Suppose it to be the Queen of Spades. Put it face up third from the left in the top row, and turn up the card that it displaced.

Keep on moving the cards in this way until you turn up the Ten of Clubs. That ends the game right there and then. But you get credit for all the cards you have turned face up, and so have either a good game or a bad one.

You can have a lot of fun playing Ten of Clubs with a friend. Each player has his own pack of cards, and each keeps track of the number of cards he is able to turn face up. You can play either five or ten games, and the one who turns up the greatest number of cards is the winner. You might even score the game by allowing each player 1 point for each card he has turned up.